OUR FAVORITE FOODS

Doughnuts

by Joanne Mattern

BLASTOFF! READERS 3

BELLWETHER MEDIA • MINNEAPOLIS, MN

Blastoff! Readers are carefully developed by literacy experts to build reading stamina and move students toward fluency by combining standards-based content with developmentally appropriate text.

Level 1 provides the most support through repetition of high-frequency words, light text, predictable sentence patterns, and strong visual support.

Level 2 offers early readers a bit more challenge through varied sentences, increased text load, and text-supportive special features.

Level 3 advances early-fluent readers toward fluency through increased text load, less reliance on photos, advancing concepts, longer sentences, and more complex special features.

★ **Blastoff! Universe**

Reading Level

Grade **K**

Grades **1–3**

Grade **4**

This edition first published in 2021 by Bellwether Media, Inc.

No part of this publication may be reproduced in whole or in part without written permission of the publisher. For information regarding permission, write to Bellwether Media, Inc., Attention: Permissions Department, 6012 Blue Circle Drive, Minnetonka, MN 55343.

Library of Congress Cataloging-in-Publication Data

Names: Mattern, Joanne, 1963- author.
Title: Doughnuts / by Joanne Mattern.
Description: Minneapolis, MN : Bellwether Media, Inc., 2021. | Series: Blastoff! Readers | Includes bibliographical references and index. | Audience: Ages 5-8 | Audience: Grades 2-3 | Summary: "Simple text and full-color photography introduce beginning readers to doughnuts. Developed by literacy experts for students in kindergarten through third grade"-Provided by publisher.
Identifiers: LCCN 2020036792 (print) | LCCN 2020036793 (ebook) | ISBN 9781644874332 | ISBN 9781648341106 (ebook)
Subjects: LCSH: Doughnuts--Juvenile literature.
Classification: LCC TX770.D67 M38 2021 (print) | LCC TX770.D67 (ebook) | DDC 641.86/53--dc23
LC record available at https://lccn.loc.gov/2020036792
LC ebook record available at https://lccn.loc.gov/2020036793

Editor: Kieran Downs   Designer: Brittany McIntosh

Printed in the United States of America, North Mankato, MN.

Table of Contents

bakery

You are at a **bakery**. There are many sweets for you to choose from.

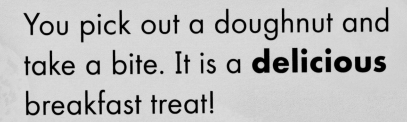

You pick out a doughnut and take a bite. It is a **delicious** breakfast treat!

Doughnuts are desserts made from **dough**. They often have a hole.

How to Make Doughnuts

1 Mix and form dough

2 Fry doughnuts

3 Top with something sweet

4 Eat and enjoy!

doughnut with custard

Doughnuts are fried in oil. They can be topped with frosting, candy, or nuts. They can also be filled with jelly or **custard**.

Doughnut History

olykoeks

Doughnuts started in the Netherlands as *olykoeks*. These were cakes with no hole in the middle. They were fried in oil.

Immigrants brought olykoeks with them to the United States in the 1700s.

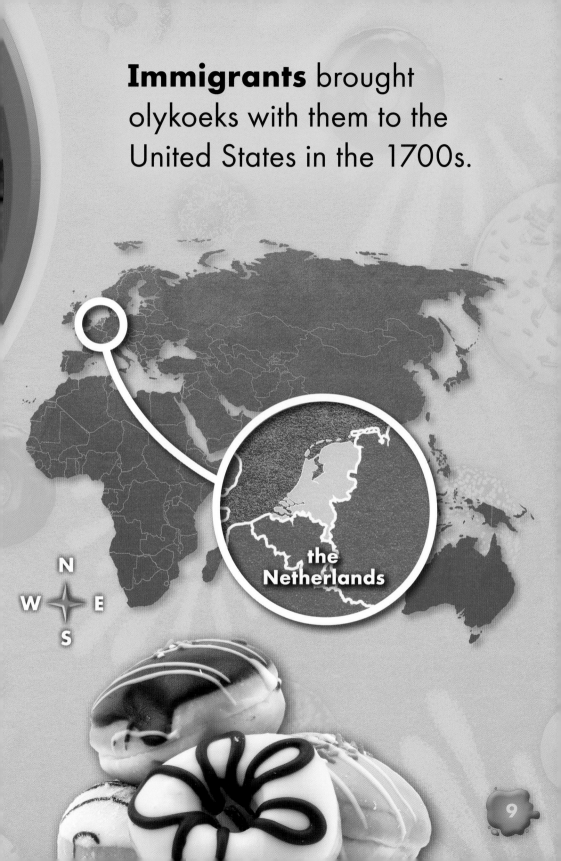

N

W   E

S

the Netherlands

Easy Doughnuts

Make this yummy treat with the help of an adult!

Tools

- large, deep frying pan
- large sandwich bag
- fork or spatula

Ingredients

- 1 package biscuit dough
- cinnamon and sugar
- vegetable oil

Instructions

1. Open the biscuit dough.

2. Separate the biscuits. Poke a hole in the middle of each one.

3. Heat the vegetable oil in a deep pan to 375 degrees Fahrenheit (191 degrees Celsius).

4. Place the doughnuts into the oil and cook for about one minute.

5. Using a fork or spatula, flip the doughnuts and cook another minute on the other side.

6. Drain the doughnuts on a paper towel.

7. Place each doughnut in the bag with cinnamon and sugar. Seal the bag and shake until the doughnuts are coated.

Doughnuts got their holes at sea. In the 1800s, a sailor named Hanson Gregory used a pepper lid to take out the middle of a doughnut. This let the doughnut cook all the way through!

In 1917, American soldiers went to France to fight in **World War I**. There, **volunteers** served the soldiers doughnuts.

Doughnut Timeline

late 1700s

Dutch people bring olykoeks to America

mid 1800s

Hanson Gregory punches a hole in a doughnut

1917

American soldiers enjoy doughnuts during World War I

making doughnuts during World War I

When the soldiers came home, they wanted more doughnuts. Bakeries started selling these treats.

Doughnuts Today

Today, doughnuts are very popular. There are about 25,000 doughnut shops in the United States.

Americans eat more than 10 billion doughnuts each year. That is enough to go around Earth 19 times!

doughnut shop

glazed
blueberry doughnuts

Doughnuts can have many different flavors. **Glazed** doughnuts are the most popular.

Some doughnuts are filled. Some are plain. Others have fruit like apples or blueberries added to the dough.

Types of Doughnuts

There are many kinds of doughnuts! Which is your favorite?

long john

doughnut hole

old fashioned

raised

People everywhere love doughnuts. In 2012, bakers in Ukraine used more than 7,000 doughnuts to make a doughnut **mosaic**.

Ukrainian doughnuts

German
doughnuts

In 2014, German bakers made
a line of doughnuts more than
1,840 feet (561 meters) long!

Doughnuts have their own holiday! National Doughnut Day is the first Friday in June. This day started in Chicago in 1938. It honors the volunteers in World War I. Celebrate with your favorite doughnut!

Sweet Glazed Doughnuts

Glazed doughnuts are the most popular doughnuts. These treats are made by covering the doughnut with liquid sugar. Ask an adult to help you make this recipe.

Tools

- large bowl
- wire rack

Ingredients

- 2 cups powdered sugar
- 1/4 cup milk
- 1 teaspoon vanilla
- 12 plain doughnuts

Instructions

1. Mix the powdered sugar, milk, and vanilla in a large bowl to make a glaze.

2. Dip the plain doughnuts into the glaze to coat them.

3. Place the doughnuts on a wire rack, and let the glaze harden.

Glossary

bakery—a store where bread and cakes are sold

custard—a sweet sauce made of milk, eggs, and sugar

delicious—very tasty

dough—a thick mixture of mostly flour and liquid

glazed—coated with liquid sugar

immigrants—people who move to another country

mosaic—a picture made of small objects

volunteers—people who do work for no pay

World War I—the war fought from 1914 to 1918 that involved many countries

To Learn More

AT THE LIBRARY

Kim, Heather. *I Donut Dare You! Bold Breakfast-Inspired Desserts for Anytime*. North Mankato, Minn.: Compass Point Books, 2019.

Leaf, Christina. *Ice Cream*. Minneapolis, Minn.: Bellwether Media, 2020.

Miller, Pat. *The Hole Story of the Doughnut*. Boston, Mass.: Houghton Mifflin Harcourt, 2016.

ON THE WEB

FACTSURFER

Factsurfer.com gives you a safe, fun way to find more information.

1. Go to www.factsurfer.com.

2. Enter "doughnuts" into the search box and click Q.

3. Select your book cover to see a list of related content.

Index

The images in this book are reproduced through the courtesy of: Guzel Studio, front cover; Nataly Studio, p. 3; Photology1971, p. 4; Christinlola, p. 5; MicrostockStudio, p. 6 (step 1); Shaiith, p. 6 (step 2); Gilmanshin, p. 6 (step 3); Dean Drobot, p. 6 (step 4); beats1, pp. 7, 11 (top); AppleEyesStudio, p. 7 (bottom); Nancy Beijersbergen, p. 8; takepicsforfun, p. 9; Sandra van der Steen, p. 10; Vintagerie Ephemera Collection / Alamy Stock Photo, p. 13; savoilic, p. 14; Randy Duchaine / Alamy Stock Photo, p. 15; Marmolejos, p. 16; Duntrune Studio, p. 17 (long john); P Maxwell Photography, p. 17 (doughnut hole); Elizabeth A. Cummings, p. 17 (old fashioned); Piyato, p. 17 (raised) Tania Kitura, p. 18; Oliver Hoffmann, p. 19; iuliia_n, p. 20; nito, p. 21; Hon Vo, p. 22.